WHEn I GroW Up i Want to Be a STURGEON

And other wrong things Kids write

Compiled and edited by
GINI GRAHAM SCOTT, PhD

 SasqUatch BooKs · Seattle

Printed in Singapore by Star Standard Industries Pte Ltd.
Published by Sasquatch Books
Distributed by Publishers Group West
15 14 13 12 11 10 09 08 07 06   9 8 7 6 5 4 3 2 1

Cover design: Nina Barnett
Interior design and composition: Nina Barnett

Library of Congress Cataloging-in-Publication Data is
available.

ISBN: 1-57061-465-2

Sasquatch Books
119 South Main Street, Suite 400
Seattle, WA 98104
(206) 467-4300
www.sasquatchbooks.com
custserv@sasquatchbooks.com

INTRODUCTION

Kids often make hilarious mistakes when they get it down on paper. This book features a range of such bloopers from assignments and tests collected from elementary to high school teachers around the United States and other countries. Mistakes range from misusing words to misquoting quotes, with humorous results. I was inspired to compile the book after working as a part-time teacher and hearing educators mention some of the funny written materials turned in by their students.

Among the most common mistakes are spelling errors that result in turning one word into another: "The Greeks wanted women only for breading purposes." Another common error is substituting a more familiar word for another, as in these resolutions: "I need to increase my self-steam," "I will try to curve my bad habits." Sometimes words are invented on the spot, as in the case of a student who argued that others were experiencing "confusement" about a topic.

Sometimes the results of guess-and-go writing are both worrisome and endearing, as one third grader wrote to his teacher: "Dear Ms._____, Youo ar da best teecher I evere head."

Misunderstood meanings abound, such as when another third grade student reported in a paper that her father, a former military professional, was "medically retarded" when he was in fact "retired." Also, mix-ups occur when students try to quote or explain the meaning of common sayings, such as when one high school student observed: "We should never jump into the fire without a frying pan."

How did I get these contributions? After starting with the half-dozen books I found on the subject, visiting dozens of Web sites with postings of bloopers in different areas, and asking for permissions to cite these quotes, I mounted my own campaign to gather contributions. I created a Web site for the book at *www.kidsmistakes.com*, where I posted a changing selection of fifty recent submissions, and I sent queries to teachers and education organizations describing the project. With just a couple exceptions, the responses were extremely positive, and besides getting e-mails back with examples of mistakes, some enthused: "What a great idea!" and many told me they would pass on the request to other teachers they knew. And so word of the project spread.

While the majority of these mistakes come from the submissions of teachers and some parents and students from around the U.S. (plus a few other countries), I have included my favorites from some of the books that have become classics on language mistakes, such as the books by Richard Lederer (*Anguished English, More Anguished English, Bride of Anguished English*, and *Fractured English*). These quotations are among those identified with the attribution "Anonymous student," used when the source of the quote did not indicate the age or grade level of the student.

I found it best to contact teachers and parents directly, because when my assistant or I tried to contact principals to spread the word to their teachers, I was often told to "contact the school district for permission," and, due to privacy concerns, some administrators said they would also have to get the parents' permission before any of their children's statements could be used. (And this in spite of my using no names and such statements being posted all over the Internet.) Still, some administrators were very supportive, letting me know they would pass the information on to others in their district.

Ironically, one of the funniest responses I received was from an English professor, who advised me that not only didn't he have such mistakes himself, but he pointed out two "mistakes" in my letter. One was when I referred to "misquoting quotes"—that should be "misquoting quotations," he said—and another was when I described myself as having published "over forty books." That should be "more than forty books," he stated. But later when I spoke to a local English teacher, she assured me that my statements were in fact correct, because "language changes." So I had apparently contacted one of the "Old School" English teachers, who still teaches the classic English constructions despite a changing world.

Then there was the English teacher who politely advised me that the headline of my Web site for collecting information—Kids Mistakes—should be Kids' Mistakes. But in popular usage, the apostrophe is often dropped. When I wrote back telling her, "I've noticed a tendency to drop these apostrephe's (or is that apostrophes) in everyday writing and headlines," she commented, "Well, it is the kind of nitpicky stuff that gives us English people a bad reputation. I prefer to save my wrangling for really important issues, like allowing singular use of 'they' (I'm for it, but others want to hang me for it)."

And so, enjoy. If you have other examples of mistakes from elementary school to college students, please send them in and include your sources, where possible, since I hope to do a follow-up book. Any submissions I receive will be considered for a TV game show based on this project that's in the works. You can send them to kidsmistakes@kidsmistakes.com or to Gini Graham Scott, Kids Mistakes, c/o Changemakers, 6114 La Salle, #358, Oakland, CA 94611.

When I feel tired,
I like to take a
cat nip.

(Elementary school student)

Rome was invaded by the ballbearings.

(Anonymous student)

You hurt my self of steam.

(Middle school student)

Dear God, are you really invisible or is it just a trick?

My ant is toast and tolerant.

History calls people Romans because they never stayed in one place for very long.

2

Socrates was a famous Greek teacher who...died from an overdose of wedlock.

(Anonymous student)

I used to be a self-scented person, but then I grew up.

(High school student)

My Dad is medically retarded.

(Third grade student, in a story about her father, who is medically retired from the military)

3

They were high school sweat hearts.

(Middle school student)

I have always wished I could have been a pilgrim on the Mayflower to catch that first glimpse of the beautiful New York skyline.

(High school student)

He was studding for a test.

(Middle school student)

I like to climb on
the jungle Jim.

(Elementary school student)

When I grow up I'd like to be
a sturgeon.

(High school student)

We had a chilly cookout
in our backyard.

(Middle school student)

The President of the United States, in having foreign affairs, has to have the consent of the Senate.

(Anonymous student)

Don't waist your money on this kind of stuff.

(Middle school student)

The system of checks and balances means you have to keep a balance in the bank to write checks.

(Anonymous student)

Hundreds of years ago, Nasturtiums predicted the end of the world.

(Middle school student)

Stradivarius sold his violins on the open market with no strings attached.

(Anonymous student)

The first five books of the Bible are Genesis, Exodus, Laxatives, Deuteronomy, and Numbers.

(Elementary school student)

7

When people sing without music, it is
called Acapulco.

(Anonymous student)

The Jews had only one
God, and his name was
Yahoo.

(Elementary school student)

The plural of music instrument is
orchestra.

(Anonymous student)

In an opera, many people get stabbed,
but then they live happily ever after.

(Anonymous student)

The process of putting a president on
trial is known as impalement.

(Anonymous student)

The first commandment
was when Eve told Adam
to eat the apple.

(Elementary school student)

When a boy reaches adulthood he says
goodbye to his boyhood and looks
forward to his adultery.

(High school student)

The first commandment
is to humor thy father
and mother.

(Elementary school student)

Probably the most marvelous fugue
was the one between the Hatfields and
McCoys.

(Anonymous student)

Beethoven was so deaf he wrote loud music.

(Anonymous student)

Beethoven is most noted for his Third, Fifth, and Ninth Symphonies. I don't know what happened to the others.

(Anonymous student)

The seventh
commandment is
thou shalt not admit
adultery.

(Elementary school student)

Eve got off to a bad start, because she was made on a rib and then ate a wormy apple.

(Elementary school student)

John Sabastian Bach wrote a great many musical compositions and had a large number of children. In between, he practiced on a spinster which he kept up in his attic.

(Anonymous student)

The Egyptians were all drowned in the dessert.

(Elementary school student)

The Egyptians suffered a lot at the hands of the locusts.

(Elementary school student)

Music sung by two people at the same time is called a duel.

(Anonymous student)

Moses found the
10 Amendments in
the Burning Bush.

(Elementary school student)

Our father who art in
heaven, Howard be thy
name.

(Third grade student)

A virtuoso is a musician with real
high morals.

(Anonymous student)

The three wise men
were wise because they
knew where to go to
find Jesus in a manager.

(Elementary school student)

When doctors first start to practice,
they take the hypocrite oath to show
how they plan to help patients.

(High school student)

Jesus said that the meek will inherit the earth, but that was before the modern stock market.

(Middle school student)

It is sometimes difficult to hear what is being said in church because the agnostics are so terrible.

(Elementary school student)

The patron saint of travelers is St. Francis of the sea sick.

(Elementary school student)

This class was a religious experience for me . . . I had to take it on faith.

(Anonymous student)

Queen Elizabeth is known for her long rain.

(High school student)

While swimming in the ocean, she got caught by the undertoe.

(Middle school student)

Dear God, please send me a pony. I never asked for anything before. You can look it up.

(Elementary school student)

The amount of education you have determines your loot in life.

(Anonymous student)

The robber looked very tough and strong when he single-handedly held up the dinner.

(Middle school student)

He was known as a cereal killer.

(High school student)

A right angle is 90 degrees Farenhight.

(Anonymous student)

It was an unusual day, when the river broke the bank.

(Middle school student)

Don't count your chickens ... It takes too long.

(Fourth grade student)

The first book of the Bible is called GenUises.

(Elementary school student)

As you shall make your bed, so shall you . . . mess it up.

(Fourth grade student)

Strike while the . . . bug is close.

(Fourth grade student)

21

Never Under estimate
the power of . . .
termites.

When there's smoke,
there's . . . pollution.

Don't bite the hand
that . . . looks dirty.

I'd like to be free as a bird in the carnival of life.

(High school student)

If you lie down with the dogs . . . you'll stink in the morning.

(Fourth grade student)

The grass is always greener . . . when you leave the sprinkler on.

(Fourth grade student)

23

The grass is always
greener ... when you
put manure on it.

(Fourth grade student)

Laugh and the whole
world laughs with you,
cry and ... you have
to blow your nose.

(Fourth grade student)

24

Laugh and the world laughs with you. Cry, and someone yells, "Shut Up!"

(Fourth grade student)

The pen is mightier than the . . . pigs.

(Fourth grade student)

25

Parallel lines never meet unless you
bend one or both of them.

(Anonymous student)

A penny saved is . . .
not worth much.

(Fourth grade student)

A penny saved is nothing
in the real world.

(Fourth grade student)

Happy is the bride who . . .
gets all the presents.

(Fourth grade student)

It's always darkest
before . . . Daylight
Savings Time.

(Fourth grade student)

27

It's always darkest before . . . I open my eyes.

(Fourth grade student)

You have nothing to fear but . . . homework.

(Fourth grade student)

We have nothing to fear but . . . our principal.

(Fourth grade student)

If you can't stand the heat . . . go swimming.

(Fourth grade student)

It takes one to know one, because it takes two to tango.

(Middle school student)

Early to bed and early to rise . . . is first in the bathroom.

(Fourth grade student)

Children should be seen
and not . . . spanked or
grounded.

(Fourth grade student)

If at first you don't
succeed . . . get new
batteries.

(Fourth grade student)

30

Make hay while the son shines.

(Middle school student)

A rolling stone . . . plays the guitar.

(Fourth grade student)

When the blind leadeth the blind . . . get out of the way.

(Fourth grade student)

Home is where the house is.

(6 year old, in a newspaper contest)

No news is . . . impossible.

(Fourth grade student)

A rolling stone gathers no mess.

(Elementary school girl)

Lead Us not into temptation, but deliver Us some e-mail.

He who hesitates is last.

Children should be seen and not herd.

Familiarity breeds attempt.

(Anonymous student)

You have to be careful of a wolf in cheap clothing.

(Middle school student)

Christians have only one spouse. This is called monotony.

(Elementary school student)

Absence makes the heart go wander.

(Anonymous student)

It's better to have a bird in the hand than one that's underfoot.

(Elementary school student)

People who live in glass houses don't need any windows.

(Elementary school student)

He who hesitates could be hit
by a bus.

Dear Ms. Williams, Youo
ar da best teecher i
evere head.

A stitch in time can make your
hand sore.

You can lead a horse to
water, but you can't lead
a cow there.

(Middle school student)

I think, therefore I . . .
get a headache.

(Fourth grade student)

Necessity is the mother of
a lot of kids.

(Middle school student)

A cliché is a common expression that has become old hat.

(Middle school student)

In Confession, you have to confess something, even if it isn't true.

(Elementary school student)

He was like a fish out of water as he jumped through the hoops in his new job.

(High school student)

Only a fowl would believe
everything they read.

(Middle school student)

The two men stopped speaking
after they had a falling down.

(Middle school student)

A bird in the hand is . . .
a real mess.

(Fourth grade student)

You have to stand for something or you could get caught in a whirlpool of doubts.

(High school student)

I think you're supposed to get shot with an arrow or something, but the rest of it isn't supposed to be so painful.

(Elementary school boy, on love)

When he opened the window,
a big guest of wind came in
the door.

(Middle school student)

The climate is hottest next to the
Creator.

(Anonymous student)

Rain is saved up in cloud banks.

(Anonymous student)

47

If falling in love
is anything like
learning how to spell,
I don't want to do it.
It takes too long.

(Elementary school boy, 7)

A blizzard is when it snows sideways.

(Anonymous student)

Yesterday I kissed a
girl in a private place.
We were behind a tree.

(Elementary school boy, 7)

A monsoon is a French gentleman.

(Anonymous student)

Like an avalanche,
where you have to run
for your life.

(Elementary school boy, 9, on falling in love)

The four seasons are salt, pepper, mustard, and vinegar.

(Anonymous student)

They are just practicing for when they might have to walk down the aisle someday and do the holy matchimony thing.

(Elementary school boy, 9,
commenting on why lovers often hold hands)

The wind is like the air, only pushier.

(Anonymous student)

I look at kissing like
this: kissing is fine if
you like it, but it's
a free country and
nobody should be forced
to do it.

(Elementary school boy, 7)

45

I know one reason that kissing was created. It makes you feel warm all over, and they didn't always have electric heat or fireplaces or even stoves in their houses.

(Elementary school girl, 8)

The government of England was a limited mockery.

(Anonymous student)

Love is when a girl puts
on perfume and a boy
puts on shaving cologne
and they go out and
smell each other.

I didn't do it, because I
didn't want the other
kids in the class to
look bad.

47

Eighty-four! Because
at that age, you don't
have to work anymore,
and you can spend all
your time loving each
other in your bedroom.

(Elementary school girl, 8, on the best age for marriage)

In the Middle Ages knights fought on horses. This was called jesting.

(Anonymous student)

It's better for girls to be single but not for boys. Boys need somebody to clean up after them.

(Elementary school girl, 9)

One of the causes of the Revolutionary War was the English put tacks in their tea.

(Anonymous student)

Marriage is when you get to keep your girl and don't have to give her back to her parents.

(Elementary school boy, 6)

Be a good kisser. It might make your wife forget that you never take out the trash.

(Elementary school boy, 8)

My mother says to look for a man who is kind . . . That's what I'll do . . . I'll find somebody who's kinda tall and handsome.

(Elementary school girl, 8, on deciding whom to marry)

A virgin forest is a forest where the hand of man has never set foot.

(Anonymous student)

You have to be careful when you
travel in the Mid East because of
the gorillas on the streets.

(High school student)

The porcupine is Known
for its pines.

(Elementary school student)

When we went to Turkey, we visited a
bizarre.

(High school student)

In some rocks we find the fossil
footprints of fishes.

(Anonymous student)

I loaned it to a friend,
but he suddenly moved
away.

(Elementary school student, on homework)

Talc is found in rocks and on babies.

(Anonymous student)

A sudden wind blew it out of my hand, and I never saw it again.

(Elementary school student, on homework)

Ms. Andrews, I love you so much. You are SO buttful! Love . . .

(Third grade student)

The great wall of China was built to keep out the mongrels.

(Anonymous student)

MR._____. Thank
you for wasting your
time to teach Us more.

(Fifth grade student, in a thank you note
to a parent who came to speak to the children
about the presidential election process)

Joan of Arc was burnt to a steak.

(Anonymous student)

I put it in a safe, but
lost the combination.

(Elementary school student, on homework)

A THANK YOU TO THE MANY SOURCES FOR THIS BOOK

This book would not have been possible without the hundreds of contributors I contacted—people with humorous lists of kids' mistakes on their Web sites; teachers who responded to my e-mails, phone calls, and requests at meetings for funny lines from their students; parents who provided humorous quotations from their kids; and several authors of books on mistakes in English who kindly permitted me to include a few of the funniest lines from their books, among them Richard Lederer, who has included chapters on kids' mistakes in several of his books—*Anguished English, More Anguished English, Bride of Anguished English,* and *Fractured English*—which I read while compiling this collection. Plus I received much encouragement from many teachers and writers, including several college professors whose material wasn't included in this first collection because it featured mistakes by college and university students, such as from Anders Henriksson, author of *Non Campus Mentis: World History According to College Students* and William W. Betts Jr., author of *Slips that Pass in the Night.*

I have tried to include everyone who provided contributions, whether they have been included in the final selection in this book or not. I also want to note that sometimes contributions came from multiple sources, since in today's Internet age, great lines get passed around by e-mail or added to personal Web sites, but sometimes the original source isn't cited. Where possible, I have tried to determine the initial contributor or book author who first cited these lines.

So here goes. Many, many thanks to:

Authors
William W. Betts Jr., author of *Slips that Pass in the Night*
Anders Henriksson, author of *Non Campus Mentis*
Richard Lederer, author of *Anguished English, More Anguished English, Bride of Anguished English,* and *Fractured English*
F.A. de Caro, Chapter 8, "Riddles and Proverbs" in *Folk Groups and Folklore Genres* by Elliott Oring
Jan Harold Brunvand, *The Study of American Folklore,* p. 106

Teachers, parents, Web site writers, and others

David E. Goldwebber
Carol Nielson
Joe Schall
Jamal Abdul-Alim
Datagirl
Lori-Ann Willey
Lynn Ann
Jim Moore
Val Perry
Dawn Shelly
Flix Productions
Richard Steinitz
Judy Music
Kenneth Quinnell
Helen Yates
Tom Brickwell
Jack Pillemer
Natasha Sarkisian
Karie Ehrlich
Gary L. Brasher
Rebecca Van Der Meer
Rochelle Riservato
Share Brownilocks

Genia Berman
Cambridge Development
   Lab
Jami Hemmenway
Wendy Irwing
Robert O'Shea
Indian Child
Tom Guthery IV
Sam, Rinkworks
Robert Hartwell
Nancee Belshaw
HN Miller
Net Jeff
Jon Schell
RRTeach
Bill Keel
Lorraine Sherry
Karen Yu
James Dignan
Jo and Tom Brickwell,
   Tech-Sol Net
Slinkycity.com
Paco Hope

Romance stuck.com
Linda and Rich Hemphill,
   Butlerwebs.com
Joel Ray
Juuky
Brian Kenny
Mapie
Lisa Collier Cool
Tom Brickwell
Jack Pillemer
Jim Moore
Owain F. Carter
Lori Mishmash
Howard Dunn
Lesly Vick
Ed Fackler
Naomi Sobel
Sharon Tzur
John Barefield
Karie Ehrlich
Lynn Ann
Mary Beth Collins
Cheryll Darnell

ABOUT THE AUTHOR

Gini Graham Scott, PhD, JD, is a nationally known writer, consultant, speaker, and seminar/workshop leader specializing in pop culture and lifestyles, as well as business relationships and professional and personal development. She is founder and director of Changemakers and Creative Communications & Research, and has published more than 40 books on diverse subjects.

Her books include: *Do You Look Like Your Dog?, A Survival Guide for Working with Bad Bosses, A Survival Guide for Working with Humans, Resolving Conflict, The Empowered Mind*, and *Mind Power*. She has received national media exposure for her books, including appearances on *Good Morning America* and *Oprah*. She has written a dozen screenplays (several under option) and has been a game designer, with more than two dozen games on the market with major game companies, including Hasbro, Pressman, and Briarpatch.

She has taught at several colleges, including California State, East Bay and Notre Dame de Namur University. She received a PhD in sociology from the University of California in Berkeley, a JD from the University of San Francisco Law School, and an MA in anthropology and in mass communications and organizational, consumer, and audience behavior from Cal State, East Bay. She is also the founder and director of PublishersAndAgents.net and the Business Connection.org, which connect writers and others with publishers, agents, the film industry, the game and toy industries, the media, and other industries.

For more information, her Web site *www.ginigrahamscott.com* includes a video of media clips and speaking engagements, and *www.giniscott.com* features her books.